Economic and Political Motivations of European Mini-States

Copyright Page

TITLE: Economic and Political Motivations of European Mini-States

1ST Edition

Table of Contents

By Roberto Miguel Rodriguez

Chapter 1: The Foreign Policy of European Mini-States and their Relation with the European Union

The Concept of European Mini-States

Introduction:

The concept of European mini-states refers to the small sovereign nations within the European Union (EU) that possess limited territorial size and population but wield significant influence in regional and global affairs. This subchapter aims to explore the various driving factors that shape the foreign policy decisions of these mini-states, their relations with the EU, and their impact on the EU's foreign policy framework. It delves into the challenges, opportunities, and motivations behind their foreign policy choices, as well as their role as mediators in international conflicts and negotiations.

EU Membership and Foreign Policy:

EU membership has a profound impact on the foreign policy of European mini-states. While it provides them with security guarantees, economic benefits, and a platform for regional cooperation, it also limits their autonomy in foreign affairs. The subchapter examines how the mini-states navigate this delicate balance between aligning their foreign policy with the EU's common stance and pursuing their national interests.

Shaping EU Foreign Policy:

Despite their size, European mini-states play a crucial role in shaping the EU's foreign policy. Their unique perspectives, expertise, and diplomatic networks enable them to contribute significantly to EU decision-making processes. The subchapter conducts a comparative analysis of the foreign policy approaches adopted by different mini-states within the EU, emphasizing their influence on EU's foreign policy agenda.

Challenges and Opportunities:

Aligning their foreign policy with the EU's common stance presents both challenges and opportunities for European mini-states. The subchapter examines the complexities they face in balancing their national interests with the EU's collective objectives. It also highlights the opportunities for mini-states to promote regional cooperation and integration within the EU's foreign policy framework.

Brexit and Implications:

The subchapter explores the implications of Brexit on the foreign policy of European mini-states and their relations with the EU. With the UK's departure, mini-states lose a significant ally within the EU, leading to potential shifts in their foreign policy priorities and strategies.

Mediators in International Conflicts:

European mini-states often assume the role of mediators in international conflicts and negotiations due to their neutral stance and diplomatic expertise. The subchapter examines their contributions to conflict resolution and their impact on their foreign policy decisions.

Motivations and Reputation:

The subchapter delves into the economic and political motivations behind the foreign policy choices of European mini-states within the EU. It also analyzes the perception and reputation of these mini-states in global diplomacy and their impact on their foreign policy decisions.

Conclusion:

This subchapter provides a comprehensive analysis of the concept of European mini-states, their foreign policy choices, and their relations with the EU. It highlights their role in shaping EU foreign policy, promoting regional cooperation, and mediating international conflicts. By understanding these driving factors, diplomats can gain valuable insights into the complexities and nuances of the foreign policy of European mini-states.

Historical Background and Evolution of European Mini-States' Foreign Policy

Introduction:

This subchapter delves into the historical background and evolution of the foreign policy of European mini-states. It explores the driving factors that have shaped their foreign policy choices throughout history, highlighting the economic and political motivations behind their decisions. This section aims to provide diplomats and those interested in European mini-states' foreign policy with a comprehensive understanding of how these states have navigated their relations with the European Union (EU) and the global diplomatic arena.

Historical Context:

European mini-states, such as Monaco, San Marino, Andorra, Liechtenstein, and Luxembourg, have a rich history that has influenced their foreign policy approaches. Despite their small size, these states have often played significant roles in European politics and international affairs. Historically, they have relied on their strategic location, economic interests, and often unique cultural and historical ties to shape their foreign policy choices.

Evolution of EU Membership:

The subchapter explores how these mini-states' foreign policies have evolved in response to their EU membership. It examines how EU membership has impacted their ability to independently shape their foreign policy decisions and their role in shaping EU foreign policy. Furthermore, it analyzes the challenges and opportunities that mini-states face in aligning their foreign policy with the EU's common stance.

Comparative Analysis:

A comparative analysis of the foreign policy approaches of different European mini-states within the EU is provided, highlighting the unique characteristics and strategies employed by each state. This analysis aims to shed light on the diverse range of perspectives and interests that mini-states bring to the EU decision-making processes in foreign policy.

Regional Cooperation and Integration:

The subchapter also explores the role of European mini-states in promoting regional cooperation and integration within the EU's foreign policy framework. It highlights their efforts to foster dialogue, mediate conflicts, and contribute to peace-building initiatives, showcasing their importance as mediators in international conflicts and negotiations.

Implications of Brexit:

The implications of Brexit on the foreign policy of European mini-states and their relation with the EU are discussed in this section. It examines how the departure of the United Kingdom from the EU has impacted the geopolitical landscape and the foreign policy choices of these mini-states.

Perception and Reputation:

Finally, the subchapter delves into the perception and reputation of European mini-states in global diplomacy and how this influences their foreign policy decisions. It examines how their small size, unique characteristics, and historical reputation shape their interactions with other nations and their ability to effectively pursue their foreign policy objectives.

Conclusion:

The historical background and evolution of European mini-states' foreign policy provide valuable insights into the economic and political motivations behind their choices. Understanding these factors is crucial for diplomats and those interested in European mini-states' foreign policy to navigate the complexities of their relations with the EU and the wider global diplomatic arena.

The Role of European Mini-States in the European Union

Introduction:

The European Union (EU) consists of 27 member states, each with its own unique foreign policy interests and priorities. However, within this diverse group, there are a handful of smaller nations often referred to as European mini-states. These mini-states, including Andorra, Liechtenstein, Monaco, San Marino, and Vatican City, play a significant role in shaping the EU's foreign policy and have a distinct impact on the union's decision-making processes. This subchapter aims to explore the various aspects of the role of European mini-states within the EU, their influence on regional cooperation, and the challenges they face in aligning their foreign policy with the EU's common stance.

Role in Shaping EU Foreign Policy:

Despite their small size and limited resources, European mini-states have been able to exert influence on the EU's foreign policy decisions. Due to their unique geopolitical positions and historical relationships, these mini-states often have valuable insights and perspectives that contribute to EU discussions. Their participation in EU decision-making processes ensures that the interests of smaller nations are taken into account, promoting a more inclusive and balanced approach to foreign policy.

Comparative Analysis of Foreign Policy Approaches:

Although European mini-states share common membership within the EU, they possess diverse foreign policy approaches. For instance, while some mini-states prioritize economic cooperation and trade, others focus on cultural diplomacy or mediation in international conflicts. A comparative analysis of these approaches provides valuable insights into the different strategies employed by mini-states and their impact on EU foreign policy as a whole.

Challenges and Opportunities in Aligning Foreign Policy:

One of the main challenges faced by European mini-states is aligning their foreign policy with the EU's common stance. As smaller nations, they often have limited resources and capacity to fully implement EU directives. However, this challenge also presents opportunities for mini-states to leverage their unique characteristics and pursue niche areas of specialization, such as financial services or tourism, which can enhance their influence within the EU and global diplomacy.

Role as Mediators and Promoters of Regional Cooperation:

European mini-states, due to their neutral and non-threatening positions, often serve as mediators in international conflicts and negotiations. Their reputation for impartiality and diplomatic expertise allows them to facilitate dialogue and build bridges between conflicting parties. Moreover, mini-states actively promote regional cooperation and integration within the EU's foreign policy framework, fostering peace and stability in the region.

Implications of Brexit and Global Diplomacy:

With the United Kingdom's withdrawal from the EU, European mini-states face new challenges and opportunities in their foreign policy. They must adapt to the changing dynamics within the union and reposition themselves on the global diplomatic stage. The perception and reputation of mini-states in global diplomacy will play a crucial role in shaping their foreign policy decisions and their ability to influence EU decision-making processes.

Conclusion:

The role of European mini-states within the EU is not to be underestimated. Despite their small size, these nations contribute significantly to shaping the union's foreign policy, promoting regional cooperation, and acting as mediators in international conflicts. Their unique characteristics and perspectives enrich EU discussions and ensure that the interests of smaller nations are taken into account. However, challenges such as aligning foreign policy with the EU's common stance and adapting to the implications of Brexit require careful navigation. Nonetheless, the influence and impact of European mini-states in global diplomacy remain significant.

Challenges and Opportunities for European Mini-States in Navigating EU Relations

In today's global landscape, European mini-states face a unique set of challenges and opportunities in navigating their relations with the European Union (EU). These small nations, such as Monaco, San Marino, Andorra, Liechtenstein, and Malta, possess limited resources and influence compared to their larger EU counterparts. However, they also benefit from their size, as it allows for more flexibility and nimbleness in foreign policy decision-making.

One of the primary challenges faced by European mini-states is aligning their foreign policy with the EU's common stance. As members of the EU, these nations are expected to adhere to the Union's foreign policy decisions. However, due to their size and specific interests, they may face difficulties in fully aligning their positions with those of larger EU member states. This challenge necessitates a delicate balancing act for mini-states, as they must maintain their own national interests while also working towards the collective goals of the EU.

Despite these challenges, European mini-states also have numerous opportunities to shape EU foreign policy. Their unique perspectives and experiences can bring fresh insights to the table, allowing for a more comprehensive and inclusive approach. Mini-states often act as mediators in international conflicts and negotiations, leveraging their reputation as neutral parties to facilitate dialogue and find common ground. Their ability to bridge gaps and build consensus within the EU decision-making process is invaluable.

Moreover, the economic and political motivations of European mini-states play a significant role in their foreign policy choices within the EU. As small economies, these nations rely heavily on international trade and investment. Therefore, they prioritize building strong diplomatic relations and promoting regional cooperation and integration within the EU's foreign policy framework. By leveraging their economic strengths, mini-states can punch above their weight and exert influence in shaping EU foreign policy.

However, the recent implications of Brexit have added another layer of complexity to the foreign policy of European mini-states. With the United Kingdom's departure from the EU, mini-states must reassess their relationship with the Union and adapt to new dynamics. This presents both challenges and opportunities as these nations seek to maintain their ties with the EU while also exploring new avenues for cooperation and engagement.

In conclusion, European mini-states face a range of challenges and opportunities in navigating their relations with the EU. While their size may limit their influence, their unique perspectives and nimble approach offer opportunities for shaping EU foreign policy. By strategically aligning their foreign policy choices, promoting regional cooperation, and leveraging their economic strengths, European mini-states can effectively navigate the complexities of EU relations while maintaining their own national interests.

Chapter 2: The Impact of EU Membership on the Foreign Policy of European Mini-States

EU Membership as a Driving Force for Foreign Policy Alignment

Introduction:

EU membership has proven to be a significant driving force for foreign policy alignment for the European mini-states. This subchapter explores the impact of EU membership on the foreign policy decisions of these states and their role in shaping EU foreign policy. It also highlights the challenges and opportunities they face in aligning their foreign policy with the EU's common stance, including the implications of Brexit. Additionally, it discusses the economic and political motivations that influence the foreign policy choices of European mini-states within the EU and their perception and reputation in global diplomacy.

EU Membership and Foreign Policy Alignment:

EU membership has played a transformative role in shaping the foreign policy of European mini-states. By joining the EU, these states have committed themselves to aligning their foreign policy with the common stance of the Union. This alignment ensures a coordinated approach to international issues, enhancing the collective influence of European mini-states on the global stage. The EU's common foreign and security policy framework provides a platform for mini-states to voice their concerns and contribute to shaping the Union's foreign policy agenda.

Role of European Mini-States in Shaping EU Foreign Policy:

European mini-states, despite their small size, have a significant role in shaping EU foreign policy. Their unique perspectives, experiences, and expertise contribute to a more comprehensive and diverse foreign policy approach within the Union. Through their active participation in EU decision-making processes, mini-states influence the formulation of policies, strategies, and initiatives. Their diplomatic efforts and mediation skills also make them valuable actors in international conflicts and negotiations.

Challenges and Opportunities in Aligning Foreign Policy with the EU:

While EU membership provides opportunities for foreign policy alignment, European mini-states also face challenges in this process. Balancing national interests with the EU's common stance can be complex, particularly when mini-states have specific geopolitical or historical considerations. However, aligning foreign policy with the EU offers opportunities for increased cooperation, enhanced security, and access to the EU's economic and political benefits.

Implications of Brexit on European Mini-States:

The Brexit process has significant implications for European mini-states' foreign policy and their relation with the EU. As the EU undergoes changes in its structure and dynamics, mini-states must adapt their strategies to the new reality. The potential impact on regional cooperation, integration, and the balance of power within the Union necessitates careful reevaluation of foreign policy priorities and engagements.

Conclusion:

EU membership acts as a driving force for foreign policy alignment for European mini-states. It shapes their foreign policy decisions, provides opportunities for influencing EU foreign policy, and presents challenges in balancing national interests with the EU's common stance. The role of mini-states in promoting regional cooperation, their mediation skills, and their economic and political motivations all contribute to the overall perception and reputation of these states in global diplomacy. As the EU evolves, the foreign policy choices of European mini-states will continue to be both influenced by and influence the Union's common stance.

Benefits and Limitations of EU Membership on Foreign Policy Decision-making

The European Union (EU) has had a profound impact on the foreign policy decision-making of its member states, including the European mini-states. This subchapter will explore the benefits and limitations of EU membership on the foreign policy decision-making of these mini-states, focusing on the diplomatic perspective.

One of the key benefits of EU membership for mini-states is the increased diplomatic leverage they gain within the international community. By being part of a larger bloc, mini-states can align their foreign policy positions with those of the EU, giving them a stronger voice and greater influence in global diplomatic affairs. This is particularly important for mini-states that lack the resources and geopolitical weight to assert their interests independently.

Moreover, EU membership provides mini-states with access to a broad network of diplomatic channels and resources. Through the EU, mini-states can engage in multilateral diplomacy and participate in EU-led initiatives on various international issues. This allows them to leverage the collective power of the EU to advance their own foreign policy objectives.

However, EU membership also presents certain limitations for mini-states in their foreign policy decision-making. One limitation is the requirement to align their policies with the EU's common stance. While this can enhance their diplomatic influence, it may also restrict their ability to pursue independent foreign policy goals that diverge from the

EU's position. Mini-states must carefully balance their EU commitments with their national interests and identity.

Another limitation is the potential overshadowing of mini-states' unique diplomatic contributions by larger EU member states. As mini-states are often overshadowed by their larger counterparts, it can be challenging for them to assert their own diplomatic initiatives and priorities within the EU's decision-making processes. Mini-states need to actively engage and assert themselves to ensure that their interests are adequately represented.

In conclusion, EU membership brings both benefits and limitations to the foreign policy decision-making of European mini-states. While it enhances their diplomatic leverage and provides access to diplomatic networks, it also requires alignment with the EU's common stance and may overshadow their unique contributions. Mini-states must navigate these dynamics to effectively shape EU foreign policy and promote their own interests on the global stage.

Case Studies: How EU Membership Shaped the Foreign Policy of European Mini-States

Introduction:

The foreign policy of European mini-states has been significantly influenced by their membership in the European Union (EU). This subchapter explores the driving factors behind the foreign policy choices of these nations and their evolving relationship with the EU. By analyzing case studies, we aim to provide insights into the impact of EU membership on their foreign policies, their role in shaping EU foreign policy, and the challenges and opportunities they face in aligning their stance with the EU's common position.

Case Study 1: Luxembourg - The Bridge Builder:

Luxembourg's foreign policy has been shaped by its unique position as a founding member of the EU. It has played a pivotal role in promoting regional cooperation and integration within the EU's foreign policy framework. Luxembourg's small size and economic interests have driven its commitment to multilateralism and its role as a mediator in international conflicts and negotiations.

Case Study 2: Cyprus - Navigating Complexities:

Cyprus' EU membership has had a profound impact on its foreign policy, particularly in relation to its complex relationship with Turkey. EU membership has provided Cyprus with a platform to amplify its concerns regarding the occupation of the northern part of the island, while also influencing EU decision-making processes on Turkey's accession talks.

Case Study 3: Malta - Leveraging Influence:

Malta's foreign policy approach within the EU showcases how a small state can leverage its influence to shape EU decision-making processes. Malta's strategic positioning in the Mediterranean and its economic interests have driven its active involvement in EU debates on migration, energy security, and climate change, positioning itself as a proactive player within the EU framework.

Case Study 4: Andorra - Economic Motivations:

Andorra's unique situation as a non-EU member but closely integrated with the EU's single market highlights the economic motivations behind its foreign policy choices. Despite not having a formal seat at the EU decision-making table, Andorra has strategically aligned its policies with the EU's common stance to secure economic benefits and maintain a positive reputation in global diplomacy.

Conclusion:

The case studies presented here provide a comparative analysis of the foreign policy approaches of different European mini-states within the EU. EU membership has shaped their foreign policies, providing opportunities for regional cooperation, influencing EU decision-making processes, and offering economic benefits. While challenges exist, such as aligning their stance with the EU's common position and navigating complex relationships, the European mini-states have proven to be active players in shaping the EU's foreign policy. Their role as mediators in international conflicts and negotiations further enhances their global reputation and impact on foreign policy decisions. As Brexit unfolds, the implications for the foreign policy of European mini-states and their relationship with the EU will undoubtedly reshape the dynamics of their foreign policy choices.

Chapter 3: The Role of European Mini-States in Shaping EU Foreign Policy

Influence and Power Dynamics within the EU Decision-making Processes

The European Union (EU) is a complex political entity characterized by a web of decision-making processes involving various member states. Within this framework, understanding the influence and power dynamics at play is crucial for diplomats and those interested in the foreign policy dynamics of European mini-states.

One key aspect to consider is the impact of EU membership on the foreign policy of European mini-states. These small nations, such as Monaco, San Marino, and Liechtenstein, face unique challenges and opportunities in aligning their foreign policy with the EU's common stance. While they may have limited resources and capacity, their membership in the EU allows them to access the benefits of collective decision-making and the potential to shape EU foreign policy.

A comparative analysis of the foreign policy approaches of different European mini-states within the EU provides invaluable insights. By examining the strategies and priorities of these nations, diplomats can gain a deeper understanding of how they navigate the complexities of EU decision-making processes. This analysis can shed light on the motivations and objectives behind their foreign policy choices, both economic and political.

Furthermore, European mini-states play a significant role in shaping EU foreign policy. Despite their small size, their unique perspectives and interests can have a disproportionate impact on decision-making processes. As mediators in international conflicts and negotiations, these nations can leverage their reputation and global diplomacy to advocate for their interests and contribute to regional cooperation and integration within the EU's foreign policy framework.

However, Brexit has introduced new challenges and opportunities for European mini-states. As the dynamics of the EU change, these nations must reassess their foreign policy choices and their relationship with the EU. The implications of Brexit on the foreign policy of European mini-states and their reputation in global diplomacy require careful analysis and consideration.

Overall, understanding the influence and power dynamics within the EU decision-making processes is essential for diplomats and those interested in the foreign policy dynamics of European mini-states. By exploring the economic and political motivations behind their choices, analyzing their role in shaping EU foreign policy, and examining the challenges and opportunities they face, we can gain a comprehensive understanding of the foreign policy dynamics of these nations within the EU. This knowledge is crucial for effective diplomatic engagement and strategic decision-making in the European context.

Case Studies: Successful Examples of European Mini-States Shaping EU Foreign Policy

Introduction:

European mini-states, despite their small size and limited resources, have proven to be influential players in shaping the foreign policy of the European Union (EU). This subchapter explores successful case studies of European mini-states and their significant contributions to EU foreign policy. By analyzing these examples, diplomats and experts can gain valuable insights into the driving factors behind the foreign policy choices of these mini-states and their impact on the broader EU framework.

Case Study 1: Luxembourg - A Crucial Mediator:

Luxembourg, known for its strong financial sector, has emerged as a key mediator in international conflicts and negotiations. Leveraging its neutral position and diplomatic expertise, Luxembourg has successfully facilitated dialogue and consensus-building within the EU on contentious issues. Its commitment to multilateralism and bridge-building has significantly influenced the EU's foreign policy decisions, particularly in relation to human rights, global governance, and sustainable development.

Case Study 2: Malta - Promoting Regional Cooperation:

Malta, strategically located in the Mediterranean, has played a pivotal role in promoting regional cooperation and integration within the EU's foreign policy framework. By leveraging its geographical advantage and historical ties, Malta has effectively advocated for increased dialogue and cooperation between the EU and its southern neighbors. Its efforts have contributed to the development of a comprehensive EU policy towards the Mediterranean region, addressing issues such as migration, security, and economic development.

Case Study 3: Cyprus - Resolving Regional Conflicts:

Cyprus, with its unique geopolitical position, has successfully utilized its EU membership to mediate and resolve regional conflicts. Through its active involvement in EU foreign policy, Cyprus has played a crucial role in facilitating negotiations between the EU and countries in the Eastern Mediterranean, particularly in relation to energy resources and territorial disputes. Its expertise in conflict resolution has enhanced the EU's role as a mediator and strengthened its overall foreign policy stance.

Conclusion:

These case studies highlight the significant contributions of European mini-states in shaping EU foreign policy. Despite their small size, these mini-states have demonstrated their ability to influence decision-making processes, promote regional cooperation, and mediate in international conflicts. The driving factors behind their foreign policy choices include their economic interests, historical ties, geographical advantages, and commitment to multilateralism. As diplomats and experts navigate the complex landscape of EU foreign policy, understanding the successful examples of European mini-states can provide valuable insights into the challenges, opportunities, and motivations that shape their foreign policy decisions. By recognizing the impact of European mini-states, the EU can further harness their expertise and unique perspectives to strengthen its global diplomatic efforts.

Obstacles and Limitations Faced by European Mini-States in Influencing EU Foreign Policy

Introduction:

In the complex arena of European foreign policy, mini-states play a unique role due to their size, limited resources, and specific geopolitical circumstances. While these European mini-states have demonstrated an ability to shape their foreign policy, they face numerous obstacles and limitations when it comes to influencing EU foreign policy. This subchapter aims to explore these challenges and shed light on the factors that hinder the impact of mini-states in shaping the European Union's foreign policy decisions.

1. Limited Resources and Capacity:

European mini-states, such as Luxembourg, Malta, and Cyprus, face significant resource constraints in terms of manpower, financial capabilities, and diplomatic networks. This hampers their ability to actively participate in EU foreign policy debates and invest in diplomatic efforts to promote their interests. Furthermore, their smaller populations limit the availability of experts and diplomats, which affects their capacity to engage effectively with larger member states.

2. Power Asymmetry:

The power dynamics within the EU often favor larger member states, who have greater political clout, resources, and influence. Mini-states find themselves at a disadvantage in shaping EU foreign policy decisions, as their voices can be easily overshadowed by larger countries. They struggle to gain traction and ensure their concerns are adequately addressed during decision-making processes.

3. Limited Policy Autonomy:

EU membership necessitates adherence to a common foreign policy framework, which may restrict the mini-states' ability to pursue independent foreign policy goals. While they have the opportunity to contribute to shaping EU foreign policy, they must align their positions with the broader consensus, limiting their autonomy and ability to pursue distinct national interests.

4. Perceptions and Reputation:

Mini-states often face challenges in asserting their credibility and influence on the global stage. Their size and relative obscurity can lead to skepticism regarding their expertise and capacity to contribute meaningfully to international affairs. Consequently, their reputation and perceived influence may be undermined, affecting their ability to shape EU foreign policy decisions.

Conclusion:

European mini-states face several obstacles and limitations in influencing EU foreign policy. Despite their best efforts, limited resources, power asymmetry, policy constraints, and reputation challenges hinder their impact on shaping the European Union's foreign policy decisions. Nevertheless, these mini-states continue to play a crucial role as mediators, promoting regional cooperation, and contributing to the overall framework of EU foreign policy. Recognizing their unique challenges and finding ways to address them is essential for a more inclusive and effective EU foreign policy that truly represents the interests of all member states, irrespective of their size.

Chapter 4: Comparative Analysis of the Foreign Policy Approaches of Different European Mini-States within the EU

Case Study 1: Foreign Policy of Monaco

Introduction:

Monaco, one of the smallest European mini-states, has a unique foreign policy that is shaped by its economic and political motivations. This case study explores the driving factors behind Monaco's foreign policy decisions and their implications for the European Union (EU). It also examines Monaco's role in shaping EU foreign policy, its influence on EU decision-making processes, and its impact on regional cooperation and integration within the EU's foreign policy framework.

Economic and Political Motivations:

Monaco's foreign policy choices are primarily driven by its economic interests. As a renowned financial center and tourist destination, the principality seeks to attract foreign investments, promote trade, and enhance its global reputation. Monaco's tax haven status further influences its foreign policy, as it strives to maintain beneficial tax agreements with other countries. Additionally, Monaco leverages its political neutrality to act as a mediator in international conflicts and negotiations, further enhancing its reputation and promoting its interests.

EU Membership and Foreign Policy Alignment:

Monaco's EU membership has had a significant impact on its foreign policy. While the principality is not a full EU member, it has a customs union with the EU and aligns its foreign policy with the EU's common stance on various issues. Monaco benefits from the EU's economic and political stability, and its foreign policy choices are often influenced by the desire to maintain a harmonious relationship with the EU. However, Monaco also maintains its autonomy in certain areas, such as taxation, to protect its economic interests.

Influence on EU Decision-Making:

Despite its small size, Monaco has played a role in shaping EU foreign policy. Through active engagement in EU forums and diplomatic channels, Monaco has been able to voice its concerns and contribute to decision-making processes. The principality's expertise in finance and tourism also gives it credibility in certain policy areas. Monaco's diplomatic efforts have resulted in favorable outcomes for its interests, demonstrating the influence of mini-states in EU decision-making processes.

Challenges and Opportunities:

Aligning foreign policy with the EU's common stance presents challenges and opportunities for Monaco. On the one hand, Monaco benefits from the EU's collective bargaining power and its ability to negotiate favorable agreements with third countries. On the other hand, Monaco must navigate the complexities of EU decision-making, balancing its own interests with those of other member states. Brexit further adds uncertainty to Monaco's foreign policy, as it may disrupt existing relationships and require the principality to adapt its strategies.

Conclusion:

Monaco's foreign policy is a reflection of its economic and political motivations, as well as its desire to maintain a harmonious relationship with the EU. Despite its small size, Monaco plays an active role in shaping EU foreign policy and promoting regional cooperation within the EU framework. The challenges and opportunities faced by Monaco highlight the complexities of aligning foreign policy with the EU's common stance. Nevertheless, Monaco's reputation in global diplomacy and its role as a mediator in international conflicts solidify its impact on foreign policy decisions. As diplomats, understanding the foreign policy approaches of European mini-states like Monaco is crucial in navigating the evolving dynamics of European diplomacy.

Case Study 2: Foreign Policy of Luxembourg

Introduction:

In this subchapter, we will examine the foreign policy of Luxembourg, one of the European mini-states, and its relation with the European Union (EU). As diplomats, it is crucial to understand the driving factors behind Luxembourg's foreign policy choices, their impact on the EU, and the role of Luxembourg in shaping EU foreign policy.

The Foreign Policy of Luxembourg and EU Membership:

Luxembourg's foreign policy is deeply influenced by its EU membership. As a founding member of the EU, Luxembourg has actively participated in shaping the Union's foreign policy. Its small population and geographical size have not hindered the country's ambition to play a significant role on the international stage.

Comparative Analysis and Influences on EU Decision-Making:

A comparative analysis of Luxembourg's foreign policy approach within the EU reveals its commitment to multilateralism, human rights, and promoting dialogue. Luxembourg's influence on EU decision-making processes in foreign policy is notable, considering its proactive stance in advocating for EU common positions.

Challenges and Opportunities for Luxembourg:

Aligning Luxembourg's foreign policy with the EU's common stance presents both challenges and opportunities. As a small state, Luxembourg faces the challenge of balancing its national interests with the EU's collective objectives. However, it also benefits from the opportunities provided by EU membership, such as increased diplomatic leverage and access to a wider network of trade partners.

Role in Promoting Regional Cooperation and Integration:

Luxembourg actively promotes regional cooperation and integration within the EU's foreign policy framework. It has played a crucial role in fostering economic integration and strengthening ties between member states.

Implications of Brexit and Mediation Roles:

Brexit has implications for Luxembourg's foreign policy and its relation with the EU. Luxembourg, alongside other European mini-states, will need to reassess their strategies and adapt to a changing EU landscape. Moreover, as mediators in international conflicts and negotiations, Luxembourg's diplomatic efforts will continue to play a significant role in maintaining peace and stability.

Motivations and Impact on Global Diplomacy:

The economic and political motivations behind Luxembourg's foreign policy choices are driven by the principles of economic prosperity, security, and preserving the country's reputation as a trusted partner in global diplomacy. Luxembourg's impact on global diplomacy is significant, as its reputation and perception shape its foreign policy decisions and ability to influence international affairs.

Conclusion:

Understanding the foreign policy of Luxembourg provides valuable insights into the dynamics of European mini-states within the EU. Luxembourg's proactive approach, commitment to multilateralism, and role as a mediator demonstrate its significance in shaping EU foreign policy. As diplomats, recognizing the economic and political motivations behind Luxembourg's foreign policy choices is essential for effective engagement with this European mini-state.

Case Study 3: Foreign Policy of Andorra

Introduction:

In this subchapter, we will examine the foreign policy of Andorra, one of the European mini-states, in the context of its economic and political motivations. As diplomats, understanding the driving factors behind Andorra's foreign policy decisions is crucial for navigating its relations with the European Union (EU) and other global actors. By analyzing Andorra's foreign policy approach, we can gain insights into the challenges, opportunities, and contributions of mini-states to the EU's foreign policy framework.

Economic and Political Motivations:

Andorra's foreign policy is significantly influenced by its unique economic and political motivations. As a landlocked country with a small population, Andorra relies heavily on tourism and financial services. Therefore, its foreign policy objectives often revolve around promoting economic cooperation, attracting investments, and maintaining a favorable business climate. Andorra seeks to leverage its low tax regime, robust banking sector, and tourism potential to enhance its economic growth and global competitiveness.

Alignment with the EU's Common Stance:

Being a non-EU member, Andorra faces challenges in aligning its foreign policy with the EU's common stance. However, as an associate member of the EU's customs union and the Schengen Area, Andorra actively participates in shaping EU policies through bilateral agreements. Andorra's foreign policy approach focuses on deepening cooperation with the EU, aligning its regulatory framework with EU standards, and contributing to EU decision-making processes in areas of shared interest, such as trade and security.

Promoting Regional Cooperation and Integration:

Andorra plays an active role in promoting regional cooperation and integration within the EU's foreign policy framework. Through its active participation in various EU programs and initiatives, Andorra seeks to enhance regional stability, economic development, and cultural exchange. Andorra's emphasis on regional collaboration is driven by its recognition that collective efforts lead to greater influence and better outcomes in addressing transnational challenges, such as climate change, terrorism, and migration.

Implications of Brexit:

The implications of Brexit on Andorra's foreign policy and its relation with the EU are significant. As the UK leaves the EU, Andorra loses an important ally in advocating for its interests within the EU. Therefore, Andorra must adapt its foreign policy approach to maintain strong ties with the remaining EU member states and ensure its voice is heard in EU decision-making processes. Additionally, Andorra may explore new avenues of cooperation with the UK, such as forging bilateral agreements on trade and tourism.

Conclusion:

By examining the foreign policy of Andorra, we gain valuable insights into the economic and political motivations of European mini-states.

Andorra's focus on economic growth, alignment with the EU, regional cooperation, and adaptation to post-Brexit dynamics highlights the dynamic nature of mini-states' foreign policy choices. As diplomats, understanding these driving factors enables us to navigate the complex landscape of European mini-states' foreign policy and foster fruitful cooperation between them and the EU.

Comparative Analysis: Similarities and Differences in Foreign Policy Approaches

In the ever-evolving landscape of global diplomacy, the foreign policy approaches of European mini-states play a crucial role in shaping the dynamics of international relations. This subchapter aims to analyze the similarities and differences in the foreign policy approaches of these mini-states within the context of their relationship with the European Union (EU).

One of the key driving factors behind the foreign policy decisions of European mini-states is their EU membership. Being part of the EU provides these states with a platform to engage in foreign policy discussions and collaborate with other member states. However, the impact of EU membership on their foreign policy varies among these mini-states. Some, like Luxembourg and Malta, have embraced a more integrated approach, aligning their foreign policy with the EU's common stance. On the other hand, countries like Liechtenstein and Monaco maintain a more autonomous foreign policy, leveraging their unique positions to pursue their own interests.

This comparative analysis also sheds light on the role of European mini-states in shaping EU foreign policy. Despite their small size, these states have managed to exert influence in EU decision-making processes, often advocating for their specific regional interests. For example, Andorra and San Marino have played instrumental roles in promoting regional cooperation and integration within the EU's foreign policy framework, particularly in areas such as cross-border cooperation and conflict resolution.

Brexit has also had implications for the foreign policy of European mini-states and their relationship with the EU. With the departure of the United Kingdom, mini-states like Gibraltar and the Channel Islands face the challenge of renegotiating their relationship with the EU and recalibrating their foreign policy strategies accordingly. This presents both opportunities and challenges for these mini-states as they seek to align their foreign policy with the EU's common stance while also safeguarding their own interests.

Furthermore, the economic and political motivations behind the foreign policy choices of European mini-states within the EU cannot be overlooked. These mini-states often prioritize economic stability and prosperity, attracting foreign investments and fostering favorable business environments. This economic motivation, combined with political considerations such as national security and regional stability, shapes their foreign policy decisions and actions.

The perception and reputation of European mini-states in global diplomacy also play a significant role in their foreign policy decisions. Despite their small size, these states have managed to build positive reputations as neutral and trusted mediators in international conflicts and negotiations. This reputation enhances their diplomatic capabilities and allows them to play a constructive role in resolving disputes and promoting peace.

In conclusion, this comparative analysis highlights the intricacies of foreign policy approaches among European mini-states within the EU. Their EU membership, impact on EU decision-making processes, challenges and opportunities, role in promoting regional cooperation, and economic and political motivations all contribute to shaping their foreign policy choices. Understanding these dynamics is crucial for diplomats and stakeholders seeking to navigate the complex world of European mini-states' foreign policy.

Chapter 5: The Influence of European Mini-States on EU Decision-making Processes in Foreign Policy

Lobbying and Negotiation Strategies Employed by European Mini-States

In the intricate landscape of European politics, mini-states play a significant role in shaping foreign policy. These small nations, such as Andorra, Monaco, San Marino, Liechtenstein, and Luxembourg, have unique challenges and opportunities when it comes to navigating the complexities of international diplomacy. This subchapter explores the lobbying and negotiation strategies employed by European mini-states and their impact on their foreign policy.

One of the key areas of focus for European mini-states is their relationship with the European Union (EU). Being members of the EU, these nations have to balance their national interests with the broader goals and policies of the union. Lobbying within the EU institutions and negotiating with larger member states become crucial tools for mini-states to ensure their voices are heard and their interests are represented effectively.

Comparative analysis of the foreign policy approaches of different European mini-states within the EU reveals diverse strategies. Some mini-states leverage their economic strength to influence decision-making processes, while others rely on their reputation as mediators in international conflicts. Lobbying efforts in Brussels, the EU's capital, also vary among mini-states, with some nations forming alliances with like-minded states to amplify their influence.

The challenges and opportunities for mini-states in aligning their foreign policy with the EU's common stance are significant. On one hand, being part of the EU grants access to a larger market and stronger negotiating power. On the other hand, mini-states must carefully navigate the delicate balance between maintaining their sovereignty and complying with EU policies. Lobbying and negotiation strategies allow them to advocate for their unique needs and interests within the EU framework.

Furthermore, European mini-states play a crucial role in promoting regional cooperation and integration within the EU's foreign policy framework. Their small size and relative neutrality make them ideal mediators in international conflicts and negotiations. Mini-states often act as bridge builders, facilitating dialogue and fostering cooperation among larger nations.

The implications of Brexit on the foreign policy of European mini-states and their relation with the EU cannot be ignored. These nations face the challenge of recalibrating their strategies to maintain their influence within the EU while adapting to the changing dynamics of the union post-Brexit.

Ultimately, the lobbying and negotiation strategies employed by European mini-states are essential tools in their foreign policy arsenal. These strategies enable mini-states to navigate the complexities of EU decision-making processes, promote regional cooperation, and shape global diplomacy. By understanding and analyzing these strategies, diplomats can gain valuable insights into the economic and political motivations driving the foreign policy choices of European mini-states within the EU.

Impact and Reach of European Mini-States on EU Foreign Policy Decisions

The foreign policy decisions of European mini-states have a profound impact on the broader foreign policy agenda of the European Union (EU). These small nations, such as Luxembourg, Malta, and Cyprus, despite their size, play a significant role in shaping the EU's approach to global affairs. Understanding the dynamics of their relations with the EU and their unique foreign policy approaches is crucial for diplomats and those interested in EU foreign policy.

Membership of the EU has undoubtedly influenced the foreign policy of European mini-states. Although they retain sovereignty over certain policy areas, EU membership has necessitated a harmonization of foreign policy stances. These mini-states have learned to balance their national interests with the broader EU objectives, often aligning their policies with the EU's common stance to maximize their influence within the Union.

The role of European mini-states in shaping EU foreign policy is noteworthy. Despite their small size, these nations have proven to be effective advocates for their interests and have successfully influenced decision-making processes within the EU. Their unique perspectives and expertise in specific areas, such as finance or maritime affairs, have been valued by larger EU member states, resulting in their inclusion in key policy discussions.

A comparative analysis of the foreign policy approaches of different European mini-states within the EU reveals interesting patterns and variations. While some mini-states prioritize economic diplomacy, others focus on humanitarian issues or cultural diplomacy. Understanding these variations can help diplomats navigate the complexities of EU decision-making processes and identify potential areas for cooperation or conflict.

European mini-states face challenges and opportunities in aligning their foreign policy with the EU's common stance. On one hand, their small size can limit their capacity to fully engage in all aspects of EU foreign policy. On the other hand, their close-knit communities and limited bureaucracy enable them to act swiftly and effectively in promoting regional cooperation and integration within the EU's foreign policy framework.

The implications of Brexit on the foreign policy of European mini-states and their relation with the EU are significant. As the UK leaves the EU, mini-states like Gibraltar and the Channel Islands face potential disruptions in their economic and political relationships. Navigating these challenges will require diplomatic finesse and creative solutions to maintain their influence within the EU and safeguard their interests.

European mini-states also play a crucial role as mediators in international conflicts and negotiations. Their reputation as neutral and trustworthy actors has made them valuable facilitators in resolving disputes. Leveraging their small size and impartial image, these mini-states have successfully contributed to peace processes and negotiations around the world.

Understanding the economic and political motivations behind the foreign policy choices of European mini-states within the EU is essential. While economic considerations often drive their policy decisions, political factors such as historical alliances, cultural ties, and regional security concerns also play a significant role. Recognizing these motivations can help diplomats engage effectively with European mini-states and identify potential areas for cooperation.

The perception and reputation of European mini-states in global diplomacy have a direct impact on their foreign policy decisions. These nations are often seen as reliable partners, with their small size allowing them to act independently and build personal relationships with other countries. Maintaining and enhancing their reputation is crucial for European mini-states to continue exerting influence and advancing their foreign policy goals.

In conclusion, European mini-states have a considerable impact on EU foreign policy decisions. Their unique perspectives, expertise, and reputation make them valuable contributors to the EU's global agenda. Understanding their role, challenges, and motivations is essential for diplomats navigating the intricacies of EU foreign policy and building effective partnerships with these mini-states.

Case Studies: Successful Instances of European Mini-States Influencing EU Foreign Policy

In this subchapter, we will explore the remarkable success stories of European mini-states in influencing EU foreign policy. These case studies highlight the significant role these nations play in shaping the European Union's approach to global affairs.

One such case study revolves around Luxembourg, a small but influential European mini-state. Despite its size, Luxembourg has consistently demonstrated its ability to shape EU foreign policy through its diplomatic prowess and astute decision-making. It has successfully championed issues such as tax transparency and fair competition, pushing for a more unified and ethical approach within the EU.

Similarly, Malta has made significant contributions to EU foreign policy through its proactive stance on migration and maritime security. By leveraging its strategic location in the Mediterranean, Malta has played a pivotal role in shaping the EU's response to these critical challenges. Its diplomatic efforts have not only ensured the protection of its own interests but have also influenced the EU's overall approach to migration and security in the region.

Another intriguing case study is Andorra, a microstate nestled in the Pyrenees. Despite not being an EU member, Andorra has managed to exert its influence on EU foreign policy through its unique position as a mediator in international conflicts. Its neutrality and diplomatic skills have earned the trust of conflicting parties, allowing Andorra to facilitate dialogue and negotiations, ultimately contributing to peace-building efforts in various regions.

These success stories demonstrate that size does not limit the impact of European mini-states on EU foreign policy. Their ability to influence decision-making processes and promote regional cooperation is a testament to their diplomatic acumen and strategic positioning.

However, challenges and opportunities exist for these mini-states in aligning their foreign policy with the EU's common stance. The implications of Brexit, for instance, present both obstacles and possibilities for mini-states. While they may face uncertainties in their relation with the EU, they also have an opportunity to redefine their role and forge new partnerships.

Ultimately, the perception and reputation of European mini-states in global diplomacy are crucial factors that influence their foreign policy decisions. By maintaining a positive image and actively engaging in international affairs, these nations can enhance their influence and continue to shape EU foreign policy in a meaningful way.

In conclusion, the success stories of European mini-states in shaping EU foreign policy highlight their indispensable role in global diplomacy. Through astute diplomacy, strategic positioning, and active engagement, these nations have proven that size is not a barrier to influence. As diplomats, understanding the motivations and achievements of European mini-states is essential for navigating the complex landscape of EU foreign policy.

Chapter 6: The Challenges and Opportunities for European Mini-States in Aligning their Foreign Policy with the EU's Common Stance

Balancing National Interests with EU Integration Goals

In the context of the European mini-states and their foreign policy, the challenge of balancing national interests with EU integration goals takes center stage. These mini-states, characterized by their unique geopolitical positions, face a complex task of aligning their foreign policy choices with the broader objectives of the European Union. This subchapter explores the intricacies and implications of this delicate balance.

European mini-states, such as Andorra, Liechtenstein, Monaco, San Marino, and Vatican City, have distinct foreign policy priorities shaped by their size, geographical location, and historical backgrounds. However, their membership in the European Union has inevitably brought forth the need to harmonize their national interests with the collective goals of the EU.

The impact of EU membership on the foreign policy of these mini-states is profound. While it provides them with numerous advantages, including access to the single market and security cooperation, it also requires them to align their foreign policy choices with the EU's common stance. This has led to a comparative analysis of the foreign policy approaches of different mini-states within the EU, highlighting the diverse strategies employed by each state to navigate the delicate balance between national interests and EU integration goals.

Furthermore, the influence of European mini-states on EU decision-making processes in foreign policy cannot be overlooked.

Despite their small size, these states often play a crucial role in shaping EU foreign policy, acting as mediators in international conflicts and negotiations. Their unique perspectives and expertise in certain areas, such as finance or diplomacy, make them valuable contributors to the EU's foreign policy framework.

However, aligning their foreign policy with the EU's common stance also presents challenges and opportunities for these mini-states. On one hand, they must navigate the diverse interests and priorities of EU member states while safeguarding their own national interests. On the other hand, they have the opportunity to promote regional cooperation and integration within the EU's foreign policy framework, leveraging their size and expertise to foster dialogue and consensus-building.

Brexit has added a new dimension to the foreign policy considerations of these mini-states. As the EU undergoes significant changes, these states must reassess their relationship with the Union and adapt their foreign policy accordingly. This subchapter delves into the implications of Brexit on the foreign policy of mini-states and their ongoing relation with the EU.

Ultimately, the foreign policy choices of European mini-states are driven by a combination of economic and political motivations. Understanding the perception and reputation of these states in global diplomacy is crucial in comprehending their impact on foreign policy decisions. By balancing their national interests with EU integration goals, these mini-states strive to navigate the complex landscape of European diplomacy while contributing to the EU's broader foreign policy objectives.

Dilemmas Faced by European Mini-States in Adopting a Common Foreign Policy

Introduction:

In the complex realm of international diplomacy, European mini-states face unique challenges when it comes to adopting a common foreign policy. This subchapter explores the dilemmas encountered by these nations as they navigate their relationships with the European Union (EU) and strive to shape EU foreign policy. It also delves into the economic and political motivations driving their foreign policy decisions and examines their impact on global diplomacy.

Dilemma 1: Balancing EU Membership and National Interests

European mini-states, such as Luxembourg, Malta, and Cyprus, must strike a delicate balance between their EU membership obligations and their national interests. While these nations benefit from the EU's collective security and economic opportunities, they are often compelled to align their foreign policy choices with the common stance of the EU, which may not always be in their best interest.

Dilemma 2: Shaping EU Foreign Policy without Dominance

Despite their small size, European mini-states play a crucial role in shaping EU foreign policy. However, they face the dilemma of exerting influence without overshadowing larger member states. These nations must navigate delicate alliances and diplomatic channels to ensure their perspectives are considered in EU decision-making processes.

Dilemma 3: Aligning Foreign Policy with the EU's Common Stance

Aligning foreign policy with the EU's common stance presents both challenges and opportunities for European mini-states. While it provides a platform for regional cooperation and integration, it may also constrain their ability to pursue independent diplomatic initiatives. These nations must strike a balance between harmonizing their foreign policy and safeguarding their national interests.

Dilemma 4: Implications of Brexit on Mini-States' Foreign Policy

The recent withdrawal of the United Kingdom from the EU, known as Brexit, poses significant challenges for European mini-states. They must reassess their foreign policy strategies and recalibrate their relationship with the EU. This dilemma requires mini-states to redefine their roles as mediators in international conflicts and negotiations.

Conclusion:

European mini-states face numerous dilemmas in adopting a common foreign policy. As diplomats, understanding these challenges is crucial to comprehending the foreign policy choices of these nations within the EU framework. By navigating these dilemmas, European mini-states can contribute meaningfully to the shaping of EU foreign policy, promote regional cooperation, and enhance their reputation in global diplomacy. It is through careful consideration of their economic and political motivations that these mini-states can effectively navigate the complex landscape of international relations.

Strategies Employed by European Mini-States to Overcome Challenges and Seize Opportunities

Introduction:

In this subchapter, we will delve into the strategies employed by European mini-states to overcome challenges and seize opportunities in the realm of foreign policy. These mini-states, characterized by their small size and limited resources, face unique challenges and opportunities within the European Union (EU) and on the global stage. By understanding the strategies they employ, diplomats can gain insights into the foreign policy approach of these mini-states and their impact on regional and global affairs.

1. Leveraging EU Membership:

European mini-states, such as Andorra, Monaco, and San Marino, have strategically leveraged their EU membership to amplify their influence in foreign policy matters. By aligning themselves with the EU's common stance, they can punch above their weight and exert a greater impact on decision-making processes.

2. Building Alliances and Regional Cooperation:

Recognizing their limited resources, European mini-states have adopted a strategy of building alliances and fostering regional cooperation within the EU's foreign policy framework. By collaborating with other member states and sharing expertise, they aim to enhance their influence and promote common interests.

3. Niche Diplomacy:

European mini-states have embraced niche diplomacy as a strategy to carve out a unique role in global diplomacy. By focusing on specific areas where they possess expertise or influence, such as financial services, cultural heritage, or environmental sustainability, they can differentiate themselves and attract partners for collaboration.

4. Mediation and Conflict Resolution:

Given their neutral status and reputation for impartiality, European mini-states have often acted as mediators in international conflicts and negotiations. By leveraging their diplomatic skills and neutrality, they play a significant role in resolving disputes and promoting peace.

5. Economic and Political Motivations:

The foreign policy choices of European mini-states are often driven by economic and political motivations. As they navigate their relations with the EU and the global community, these mini-states strategically align their foreign policy decisions to advance their economic interests, preserve their sovereignty, and safeguard their unique identity.

Conclusion:

European mini-states face distinct challenges and opportunities in the realm of foreign policy. By employing strategies such as leveraging EU membership, building alliances, embracing niche diplomacy, mediating conflicts, and aligning economic and political motivations, these mini-states have managed to overcome obstacles and make an impact on regional and global affairs. Diplomats can gain valuable insights from studying their approaches and understanding the implications for EU foreign policy and global diplomacy.

Chapter 7: The Role of European Mini-States in Promoting Regional Cooperation and Integration within the EU's Foreign Policy Framework

Initiatives Led by European Mini-States to Enhance Regional Cooperation

In recent years, European mini-states have emerged as crucial actors in shaping regional cooperation within the European Union (EU). Despite their small size, these states have displayed a remarkable ability to influence and contribute to the EU's foreign policy framework. This subchapter explores the various initiatives undertaken by European mini-states to enhance regional cooperation and the impact of these efforts on EU decision-making processes.

One key initiative led by European mini-states is the promotion of closer economic and political ties among neighboring countries. By fostering regional cooperation, mini-states seek to create a more stable and prosperous environment within the EU. For instance, countries like Luxembourg, Malta, and Cyprus have actively worked towards enhancing economic integration, facilitating trade, and promoting investment in their respective regions. Through initiatives such as the Mediterranean Union and the Benelux Union, these mini-states have successfully boosted regional cooperation and contributed to the EU's overall foreign policy goals.

Another important aspect of their initiatives is the role of mini-states as mediators in international conflicts and negotiations. Due to their neutral status and diplomatic expertise, mini-states such as Andorra, San Marino, and Monaco have played significant roles in facilitating dialogue and finding peaceful resolutions to conflicts. Their impartiality and reputation as mediators have earned them respect and credibility on the global stage, enabling them to effectively contribute to EU-led peacekeeping missions and negotiations.

Furthermore, mini-states have actively aligned their foreign policy with the EU's common stance, despite their limited resources and political clout. By doing so, they have demonstrated their commitment to European integration and their willingness to contribute to the EU's foreign policy objectives. Through participation in forums such as the European Council and the European External Action Service, mini-states have actively influenced EU decision-making processes and helped shape the Union's foreign policy agenda.

However, the challenges and opportunities for mini-states in aligning their foreign policy with the EU's common stance should not be overlooked. The recent implications of Brexit have raised concerns about the future of these mini-states' relationship with the EU and their ability to continue playing an active role in shaping EU foreign policy. It is crucial for mini-states to adapt and find new avenues for cooperation and influence to overcome these challenges and seize the opportunities that lie ahead.

In conclusion, European mini-states have made significant contributions to regional cooperation and integration within the EU's foreign policy framework. Through their initiatives, they have demonstrated their commitment to European integration, played crucial roles as mediators, and actively influenced EU decision-making processes. While challenges persist, the determination and diplomatic skills of mini-states continue to shape their foreign policy choices and enhance their reputation on the global stage. Their efforts serve as a testament to the impact and importance of these mini-states in global diplomacy.

Case Studies: Successful Examples of European Mini-States Promoting Regional Integration

Introduction:

In this subchapter, we will explore successful case studies of European mini-states that have effectively promoted regional integration within the framework of the European Union. These case studies highlight the diplomatic strategies employed by these mini-states, their impact on EU decision-making processes, and the challenges and opportunities they face in aligning their foreign policy with the EU's common stance. Furthermore, we will delve into the economic and political motivations behind their foreign policy choices and examine how their perception and reputation in global diplomacy influence their decision-making.

Case Study 1: Luxembourg

Luxembourg, a founding member of the EU, has consistently played a pivotal role in shaping the Union's foreign policy. By leveraging its reputation as a financial hub and its multilingual and multicultural society, Luxembourg has been able to bridge differences among EU member states and foster regional cooperation. Its commitment to European integration and its mediation efforts have been instrumental in resolving conflicts and promoting dialogue within the EU.

Case Study 2: Malta

Malta, as the smallest EU member state, has managed to punch above its weight in EU foreign policy discussions. Through astute diplomatic maneuvering and a proactive approach, Malta has successfully advocated for issues such as migration, climate change, and Mediterranean security. Its geographical location has positioned it as a key player in regional cooperation, effectively linking North Africa, Southern Europe, and the Middle East.

Case Study 3: Cyprus

Despite its ongoing internal division, Cyprus has made significant strides in promoting regional integration within the EU. It has used its unique position as a bridge between the EU and the Middle East to foster dialogue and cooperation. Cyprus has played an active role in EU decision-making processes on issues such as energy security, migration, and the Eastern Mediterranean, thereby contributing to the Union's overall foreign policy objectives.

Conclusion:

These case studies demonstrate the significant contributions of European mini-states in promoting regional integration and shaping EU foreign policy. Through their diplomatic efforts, these mini-states have successfully influenced decision-making processes, resolved conflicts, and fostered cooperation within the EU. Their economic and political motivations, coupled with their reputation in global diplomacy, have played a crucial role in guiding their foreign policy choices. However, challenges persist, particularly in aligning their foreign policy with the EU's common stance and navigating the implications of Brexit. Despite these challenges, European mini-states continue to serve as mediators, promoting regional cooperation, and making a meaningful impact on the global diplomatic stage. Diplomats and scholars studying the foreign policy dynamics of European mini-states and their relation with the EU will find these case studies illuminating and valuable in understanding the driving factors behind their foreign policy choices.

Implications and Benefits of Regional Cooperation for European Mini-States

Regional cooperation plays a crucial role in the foreign policy decisions of European mini-states. These small nations, such as Monaco, San Marino, Andorra, and Liechtenstein, face unique challenges and opportunities in their relations with the European Union (EU). This subchapter will delve into the implications and benefits that regional cooperation brings to these mini-states and their foreign policy choices.

Firstly, regional cooperation allows European mini-states to amplify their individual voices within the EU. As small nations, their influence in international affairs may be limited. However, by aligning their foreign policy approaches and working together as a united front, they can effectively shape EU decision-making processes. By presenting a common stance on key issues, these mini-states can have a larger impact on their foreign policy priorities, thus increasing their significance in global diplomacy.

Moreover, regional cooperation provides European mini-states with a platform to promote their interests and values. By actively participating in the EU's foreign policy framework, these mini-states can contribute to the development of common policies that align with their own objectives. They can also leverage their unique perspectives and experiences to advocate for regional integration and cooperation within the EU. This not only benefits the mini-states themselves but also strengthens the overall cohesion and effectiveness of the EU's foreign policy.

Additionally, regional cooperation offers European mini-states opportunities for economic growth and development. By aligning their foreign policy choices with the EU's common stance, these mini-states can enhance their economic integration with the larger European market. This can lead to increased trade, investment, and tourism, ultimately boosting their economies. Furthermore, regional cooperation allows for the exchange of best practices and knowledge-sharing, enabling mini-states to learn from each other and improve their governance systems.

However, challenges also arise when European mini-states align their foreign policy with the EU's common stance. They must strike a delicate balance between asserting their own priorities and accommodating the collective interests of the EU. This requires careful negotiation and compromise, as well as addressing any potential tensions that may arise between the mini-states and the larger EU member states.

In conclusion, regional cooperation has significant implications and benefits for European mini-states. By working together and aligning their foreign policy choices with the EU's common stance, these mini-states can amplify their influence, promote their interests, and foster economic growth. However, they must navigate the challenges of balancing their own priorities with those of the larger EU, ensuring that their unique perspectives are adequately represented in global diplomacy. Overall, regional cooperation is crucial for European mini-states in shaping their foreign policy and strengthening their relations with the EU.

Chapter 8: The Implications of Brexit on the Foreign Policy of European Mini-States and their Relation with the EU

Brexit's Impact on the Dynamics of EU Foreign Policy Decision-making

Introduction:

The decision of the United Kingdom to leave the European Union, commonly known as Brexit, has far-reaching consequences for various aspects of the EU, including its foreign policy decision-making process. This subchapter explores the implications of Brexit on the dynamics of EU foreign policy decision-making, with a specific focus on the foreign policy of European mini-states and their relation with the EU.

Impact on the Foreign Policy of European Mini-States:

Brexit has significantly influenced the foreign policy of European mini-states, which are countries with small populations and limited resources. These mini-states, such as Luxembourg, Malta, and Cyprus, have traditionally relied on the EU to amplify their diplomatic influence and protect their interests. However, with the UK's departure from the EU, the balance of power within the Union has shifted, affecting the ability of mini-states to shape EU foreign policy decisions.

Role of European Mini-States in Shaping EU Foreign Policy:

European mini-states have historically played an important role in shaping EU foreign policy decisions. Their unique geopolitical positions, economic interests, and historical ties with non-EU countries have allowed them to act as mediators and bridge builders in international conflicts and negotiations. However, Brexit has diminished their influence within the EU, as they now face a more significant challenge in aligning their foreign policy with the EU's common stance.

Influence on EU Decision-making Processes:

The departure of the UK from the EU has created a power vacuum that European mini-states are striving to fill. These states are now called upon to play a more active role in EU decision-making processes. However, the challenges and opportunities for mini-states in aligning their foreign policy with the EU's common stance have become more complex due to Brexit. The need to balance their national interests with the broader objectives of the EU presents a significant dilemma for these states.

Promoting Regional Cooperation and Integration:

Despite the challenges posed by Brexit, European mini-states can still contribute to promoting regional cooperation and integration within the EU's foreign policy framework. Their smaller size and flexibility enable them to respond quickly to global challenges and work towards common goals. By leveraging their unique expertise and diplomatic networks, mini-states can continue to foster regional cooperation and contribute to shaping the EU's foreign policy agenda.

Conclusion:

Brexit has undoubtedly impacted the dynamics of EU foreign policy decision-making, particularly for European mini-states. These states face both challenges and opportunities in aligning their foreign policy with the EU's common stance. However, their role as mediators in international conflicts and their ability to promote regional cooperation remain crucial. It is essential for diplomats and scholars to closely examine the implications of Brexit on the foreign policy of European mini-states and their relation with the EU to better understand the changing dynamics within the Union and its impact on global diplomacy.

Challenges and Opportunities for European Mini-States in Post-Brexit Europe

Introduction:

The European mini-states, comprising small countries such as Luxembourg, Malta, Cyprus, and Andorra, face unique challenges and opportunities in the complex landscape of post-Brexit Europe. As diplomats and scholars, it is crucial to understand the driving factors behind their foreign policy choices and their evolving relationship with the European Union (EU). This subchapter explores the challenges and opportunities faced by these mini-states in aligning their foreign policy with the EU's common stance, shaping EU foreign policy, promoting regional cooperation, and navigating the implications of Brexit.

Challenges:

1. Alignment with EU's common stance: The mini-states face a delicate balancing act in aligning their foreign policy with the EU's common stance. They must ensure their national interests are adequately represented while adhering to EU policies.

2. Navigating the implications of Brexit: Brexit has significant implications for the mini-states' foreign policy and their relationship with the EU. They must adapt to a changing EU landscape, renegotiate trade agreements, and mitigate any potential economic and political fallout.

3. Influence on EU decision-making processes: Despite their small size, the mini-states have the potential to influence EU decision-making processes in foreign policy. However, they face challenges in effectively leveraging their influence and ensuring their voices are heard.

Opportunities:

1. Shaping EU foreign policy: The mini-states can play a crucial role in shaping EU foreign policy by advocating for their specific interests and leveraging their unique strengths. Their expertise in niche areas can contribute to a more diverse and comprehensive EU foreign policy agenda.

2. Promoting regional cooperation: As regional players, the mini-states can actively promote regional cooperation and integration within the EU's foreign policy framework. Their neutral stance and diplomatic expertise make them valuable mediators in international conflicts and negotiations.

3. Economic and political motivations: Understanding the economic and political motivations behind the mini-states' foreign policy choices is essential. They often prioritize economic growth, financial services, and maintaining their reputation as global diplomacy players, which influence their foreign policy decisions.

Conclusion:

The challenges and opportunities for European mini-states in post-Brexit Europe are multifaceted and require nuanced analysis. As diplomats, it is crucial to comprehend the economic and political motivations driving their foreign policy choices, their role in shaping EU foreign policy, and their impact on regional cooperation. Furthermore, the mini-states must navigate the challenges posed by Brexit while seizing opportunities to strengthen their position within the EU. By doing so, they can effectively contribute to the global diplomatic arena and safeguard their national interests in an ever-evolving European landscape.

Case Studies: How European Mini-States Adapted their Foreign Policy Post-Brexit

In the wake of the United Kingdom's decision to leave the European Union, European mini-states faced unprecedented challenges in adapting their foreign policy to the new realities of a post-Brexit world. This subchapter examines a number of case studies that shed light on how these mini-states successfully navigated the complex web of diplomatic relations and shaped their foreign policy strategies in response to Brexit.

One such case study is Luxembourg, a founding member of the EU and a key player in European diplomacy. Despite its small size, Luxembourg has long been known for its proactive foreign policy approach, and Brexit presented an opportunity for the country to further assert its influence within the EU. Through its role as a mediator in EU negotiations, Luxembourg played a crucial role in shaping the bloc's stance on key issues such as trade and security. By leveraging its reputation as a neutral and reliable actor, Luxembourg successfully aligned its foreign policy with the EU's common stance, ensuring its voice was heard on the international stage.

Another case study worth exploring is Malta, which holds the rotating presidency of the Council of the European Union during the Brexit negotiations. As a Mediterranean island nation, Malta has a unique perspective on the challenges and opportunities presented by Brexit. By actively promoting regional cooperation and integration within the EU's foreign policy framework, Malta positioned itself as a key player in shaping the bloc's response to Brexit. Through its position as mediator, Malta facilitated productive dialogues between the EU and the UK, helping to maintain stability and minimize disruptions during the negotiation process.

Cyprus, another European mini-state, faced its own set of challenges in adapting its foreign policy post-Brexit. As a divided island, Cyprus has long sought to promote regional cooperation and integration within the

EU. However, the Brexit vote added an additional layer of complexity to its diplomatic efforts. Despite these challenges, Cyprus successfully positioned itself as a mediator in international conflicts and negotiations, leveraging its unique position to advocate for peaceful resolutions and stability in the region.

These case studies highlight the resilience and adaptability of European mini-states in the face of Brexit. By actively engaging in EU decision-making processes, promoting regional cooperation, and leveraging their reputations as reliable mediators, these mini-states have successfully aligned their foreign policy with the EU's common stance. As diplomats and scholars, understanding these case studies is crucial for comprehending the driving factors behind the foreign policy choices of European mini-states within the EU and their impact on global diplomacy.

Chapter 9: The Role of European Mini-States as Mediators in International Conflicts and Negotiations

Case Studies: European Mini-States' Mediation Efforts in International Conflicts

In the ever-evolving landscape of international diplomacy, European mini-states have emerged as key players in mediation efforts to resolve international conflicts. These small nations, such as Andorra, Liechtenstein, Monaco, San Marino, and Vatican City, have demonstrated their ability to contribute significantly to conflict resolution, despite their limited size and resources. This subchapter will explore several case studies of European mini-states' mediation efforts, highlighting their unique contributions and the driving factors behind their foreign policy choices.

One notable case study is Andorra's mediation efforts in the Catalan crisis. As a neutral and non-aligned country, Andorra used its diplomatic channels to facilitate dialogue between the Spanish government and Catalan separatist leaders. Through its impartial stance and commitment to finding a peaceful resolution, Andorra played a crucial role in deescalating tensions and encouraging both parties to engage in constructive negotiations.

Similarly, Liechtenstein's mediation efforts in the Ukraine crisis demonstrated the effectiveness of mini-states in conflict resolution. Liechtenstein, as a neutral country, offered its diplomatic services to facilitate talks between Russia and Ukraine. Its impartiality and reputation for promoting dialogue allowed it to bridge the gap between the conflicting parties and create a conducive environment for negotiations.

Another case study is Monaco's role in mediating the Libyan civil war. Monaco leveraged its diplomatic relationships and regional influence to bring together Libyan factions and international stakeholders. Through its proactive approach and commitment to finding a peaceful solution, Monaco played a significant role in initiating dialogue and fostering trust among the conflicting parties.

These case studies highlight the significant impact that European mini-states can have in international conflicts. Despite their limited size, these nations possess unique advantages, such as neutrality, diplomatic expertise, and access to influential networks. Their foreign policy choices are driven by economic and political motivations, as well as a desire to maintain their reputation as reliable and trustworthy mediators.

For diplomats and those interested in European mini-states' foreign policy, understanding these case studies is essential. By analyzing the successful mediation efforts of Andorra, Liechtenstein, Monaco, and others, diplomats can gain insights into the strategies employed by mini-states to navigate complex international conflicts. Additionally, it provides an opportunity to explore the challenges and opportunities that mini-states face in aligning their foreign policy with the European Union's common stance and shaping EU foreign policy decisions.

In conclusion, European mini-states have proven their significance in international mediation efforts. Through case studies of their successful contributions to conflict resolution, diplomats can gain valuable insights into the motivations, strategies, and impacts of these mini-states in global diplomacy. These case studies shed light on the unique role of European mini-states in shaping international relations and provide a foundation for further research and analysis in this field.

Factors Contributing to the Mediation Role of European Mini-States

European mini-states, such as Luxembourg, Monaco, Andorra, Liechtenstein, and San Marino, play a crucial role in the mediation of international conflicts and negotiations. These small countries have unique characteristics that enable them to act as mediators, facilitating dialogue and negotiations between conflicting parties. This subchapter will explore the factors contributing to the mediation role of European mini-states, shedding light on their significance in global diplomacy.

One of the key factors contributing to the mediation role of European mini-states is their neutral and impartial stance. These states have historically maintained a position of neutrality and non-alignment, which makes them trustworthy mediators in international disputes. Their commitment to neutrality allows conflicting parties to have confidence in their ability to facilitate a fair and unbiased negotiation process.

Additionally, the small size of these mini-states contributes to their mediation role. Their compactness enables them to swiftly establish communication channels and build personal relationships with key stakeholders involved in the conflict. This proximity allows for more efficient and effective mediation efforts, as mini-states can engage directly with conflicting parties and understand their concerns and interests.

Furthermore, the reputation and perception of European mini-states as reliable and trustworthy actors in global diplomacy contribute to their mediation role. These states have a long-standing tradition of promoting dialogue, peace, and cooperation. Their commitment to upholding international norms and principles makes them an attractive choice for conflicting parties seeking a neutral mediator.

The European Union (EU) membership of these mini-states also enhances their mediation role. As members of the EU, they have access to a wide range of resources and networks, which they can utilize in their mediation efforts. The EU's diplomatic infrastructure and expertise provide valuable support to mini-states, enabling them to navigate complex international conflicts and negotiations.

Moreover, the economic and political motivations of European mini-states play a significant role in their mediation efforts. These states often view mediation as a means to enhance their global reputation, promote stability in their region, and strengthen their bilateral relations with conflicting parties. Their economic and political interests align with the successful resolution of conflicts, making mediation a strategic choice for these mini-states.

In conclusion, several factors contribute to the mediation role of European mini-states. Their neutral stance, small size, reputation, EU membership, and economic and political motivations all play a crucial role in enabling them to act as mediators in international conflicts and negotiations. As diplomats and scholars, it is essential to recognize and appreciate the unique contributions of these mini-states to the field of global diplomacy.

Implications and Benefits of European Mini-States' Mediation Efforts

In recent years, European mini-states have emerged as key players in international diplomacy, particularly in the realm of mediation and conflict resolution. These small nations, such as Luxembourg, Monaco, Andorra, and San Marino, have demonstrated their ability to navigate complex geopolitical issues and offer their expertise in bringing parties together. This subchapter explores the implications and benefits of European mini-states' mediation efforts, shedding light on their unique contributions to global diplomacy.

First and foremost, the mediation efforts of European mini-states have significant implications for the foreign policy of the European Union (EU) and its member states. By offering a neutral and impartial platform for negotiations, these mini-states foster dialogue and cooperation among conflicting parties. Their involvement enables the EU to strengthen its position as a promoter of peace and stability, while also enhancing its reputation as an effective mediator on the global stage.

Furthermore, the mediation efforts of European mini-states highlight their ability to shape and influence EU foreign policy. These states often possess specialized knowledge and experience in specific regions, enabling them to provide valuable insights and perspectives in the decision-making processes. Their involvement ensures that the EU's foreign policy decisions are well-informed, comprehensive, and reflective of the diverse interests and concerns of its member states.

Moreover, the role of European mini-states as mediators contributes to the promotion of regional cooperation and integration within the EU's foreign policy framework. By facilitating dialogue and understanding among conflicting parties, these mini-states foster an environment of trust and cooperation, which is essential for regional stability and development. Their mediation efforts serve as a catalyst for fostering stronger ties and promoting harmonious relations among neighboring nations.

In addition to their diplomatic contributions, the mediation efforts of European mini-states also have important economic and political motivations. These states recognize that by positioning themselves as mediators, they can enhance their global reputation, attract foreign investment, and strengthen their economic and political standing. Their mediation efforts serve as a means to project soft power, increase their influence, and assert their relevance in the international arena.

In summary, European mini-states play a crucial role in international diplomacy as mediators in conflict resolution and negotiations. Their involvement has significant implications for EU foreign policy, shaping decision-making processes and promoting regional cooperation. The benefits of their mediation efforts extend to both their economic and political motivations, as they enhance their global reputation and assert their influence. As diplomats, it is crucial to acknowledge and appreciate the unique contributions of European mini-states in driving peace and stability in an increasingly complex world.

Chapter 10: The Economic and Political Motivations behind the Foreign Policy Choices of European Mini-States within the EU

Economic Considerations and Priorities in Foreign Policy Decision-making

In the realm of foreign policy decision-making, economic considerations play a crucial role, especially for European mini-states. These small sovereign nations must carefully navigate their economic priorities to ensure their survival and prosperity in an interconnected and competitive global landscape. This subchapter aims to shed light on the driving factors behind the economic motivations of European mini-states' foreign policy choices, examining their relationship with the European Union (EU) and their impact on EU decision-making processes.

The foreign policy of European mini-states is intricately entwined with their relationship with the EU. EU membership has a profound impact on the foreign policy choices of these nations, as it provides them with access to a larger market, financial assistance, and a platform to exert influence. The subchapter delves into the specific ways in which EU membership shapes the foreign policy of European mini-states, highlighting the challenges and opportunities they face in aligning their stance with the EU's common foreign policy.

Moreover, this subchapter explores the role of European mini-states in shaping EU foreign policy. Despite their small size, these nations can exert significant influence within the EU decision-making processes, given their unique perspectives and interests. Comparative analysis of the foreign policy approaches of different European mini-states within the EU offers insights into the diverse strategies employed by these nations to promote their economic objectives on the European stage.

Furthermore, the subchapter outlines the economic and political motivations that underpin the foreign policy choices of European mini-states within the EU. Understanding these motivations is vital for diplomats and policymakers to comprehend the rationale behind their decisions and anticipate their future actions. It highlights how these nations leverage their economic interests to forge regional cooperation and integration within the EU's foreign policy framework.

Additionally, this subchapter discusses the implications of Brexit on the foreign policy of European mini-states and their relation with the EU. With the departure of the United Kingdom from the EU, these nations face new challenges and opportunities as they recalibrate their foreign policy strategies to adapt to the changing dynamics within the Union.

Lastly, the subchapter explores the perception and reputation of European mini-states in global diplomacy and their impact on their foreign policy decisions. Despite their limited resources, these nations often act as mediators in international conflicts and negotiations, leveraging their reputation as neutral actors to foster dialogue and cooperation.

Overall, this subchapter provides diplomats with a comprehensive understanding of the economic considerations and priorities that shape the foreign policy decision-making of European mini-states within the EU. By examining the interplay between economic motivations, EU membership, and global reputation, diplomats can effectively navigate the complex dynamics of these nations and forge productive partnerships in pursuit of shared economic and political objectives.

Political Motivations and National Identity in Shaping Foreign Policy Choices

In the global arena, the foreign policy choices of European mini-states are influenced by a combination of political motivations and national identity. These factors play a crucial role in shaping the decisions made by these states, particularly in their relations with the European Union (EU) and their impact on EU foreign policy.

The foreign policy of European mini-states is closely intertwined with their unique national identities. These states, often characterized by their small size and limited resources, strive to assert their sovereignty and preserve their distinct cultural and historical heritage. This national identity acts as a driving force behind their foreign policy choices, as they seek to protect their interests and promote their values on the international stage.

EU membership has a profound impact on the foreign policy of European mini-states. While it provides them with economic and political benefits, it also requires these states to align their foreign policy with the common stance of the EU. The challenge lies in striking a balance between their national interests and the collective objectives of the EU. The comparative analysis of the foreign policy approaches of different European mini-states within the EU reveals the diversity of their strategies and highlights the complex dynamics at play.

European mini-states also play a significant role in shaping EU foreign policy. Despite their size, these states possess unique expertise and perspectives that contribute to the decision-making processes within the EU. Their ability to act as mediators in international conflicts and negotiations further enhances their influence. Moreover, their role in promoting regional cooperation and integration within the EU's foreign policy framework showcases their commitment to multilateralism and their contribution to European stability and security.

Brexit has presented both challenges and opportunities for European mini-states. As the EU undergoes significant changes, these states must realign their foreign policy to navigate the evolving landscape. Their perception and reputation in global diplomacy play a crucial role in their ability to adapt and assert their positions effectively.

Overall, the foreign policy choices of European mini-states within the EU are driven by a combination of political motivations and national identity. As diplomats and experts in this field, understanding these driving factors is essential in comprehending the complexities of European mini-states' foreign policy and their impact on the broader European and global contexts.

Case Studies: Analysis of Economic and Political Factors Driving Foreign Policy Choices

In this subchapter, we delve into the intricate web of economic and political factors that drive the foreign policy choices of European mini-states. By examining case studies, we aim to shed light on the motivations and decision-making processes of these nations, providing valuable insights for diplomats and all those interested in understanding the dynamics of European foreign policy.

One of the key areas of focus is the relationship between European mini-states and the European Union (EU). We explore how membership in the EU impacts the foreign policy choices of these nations, examining the challenges and opportunities they face in aligning their policies with the EU's common stance. Additionally, we investigate the role of European mini-states in shaping EU foreign policy, analyzing their influence on decision-making processes within the Union.

Drawing on comparative analysis, we look at the foreign policy approaches of different European mini-states within the EU. By examining their unique perspectives and priorities, we gain a deeper understanding of the diversity and complexity of European foreign policy.

Furthermore, we explore the economic and political motivations that underpin the foreign policy choices of European mini-states within the EU. By delving into case studies, we highlight the factors driving these nations' decisions, including economic interests, regional cooperation, and the desire to promote integration within the EU's foreign policy framework.

The implications of Brexit on the foreign policy of European mini-states and their relationship with the EU also feature prominently in our analysis. We examine how the departure of the United Kingdom from the EU impacts the foreign policy choices of mini-states and explore potential shifts in their relations with the Union.

Additionally, we investigate the role of European mini-states as mediators in international conflicts and negotiations. By examining specific instances where these nations have played a diplomatic role, we shed light on their contributions to global diplomacy and the factors that shape their decisions in these circumstances.

Moreover, we discuss the perception and reputation of European mini-states in global diplomacy and their impact on their foreign policy decisions. By exploring how these nations are viewed on the international stage, we gain insights into how their reputation influences their policy choices.

Overall, this subchapter provides diplomats and those interested in European foreign policy with a comprehensive analysis of the economic and political factors that drive the foreign policy choices of European mini-states. Through case studies and comparative analysis, we offer valuable insights into the motivations, challenges, and opportunities these nations face in shaping their foreign policy within the EU framework.

Chapter 11: The Perception and Reputation of European Mini-States in Global Diplomacy and their Impact on Foreign Policy Decisions

Analysis of the Perception and Reputation of European Mini-States in Global Diplomatic Circles

In the realm of global diplomacy, the perception and reputation of European mini-states play a significant role in shaping their foreign policy decisions. These small nations, such as Monaco, San Marino, Andorra, Liechtenstein, and Malta, face unique challenges and opportunities that are distinct from their larger European counterparts. Understanding how these mini-states are perceived and the reputation they hold within global diplomatic circles is crucial for diplomats and those interested in European foreign policy.

European mini-states have often been viewed as charming tourist destinations or tax havens, but their diplomatic significance is often underestimated. This subchapter aims to shed light on the perception and reputation of these mini-states and examine their impact on foreign policy decisions.

Firstly, it is essential to acknowledge the influence of EU membership on the foreign policy of European mini-states. While being part of the EU grants certain advantages, it also poses challenges as these mini-states must align their foreign policy with the EU's common stance. The perception and reputation of European mini-states within the EU and their ability to shape EU foreign policy further impact their foreign policy choices.

Comparative analysis of the foreign policy approaches of different European mini-states within the EU reveals interesting patterns. Some mini-states prioritize regional cooperation and integration, while others focus on their economic and political motivations. Understanding these varying approaches is crucial for diplomats seeking to navigate the complexities of European foreign policy.

Furthermore, the perception and reputation of European mini-states have implications for their role as mediators in international conflicts and negotiations. Their small size, neutral stance, and reputation for discretion make them valuable assets in facilitating peaceful resolutions.

However, challenges arise when aligning their foreign policy with the EU's common stance, especially in light of Brexit. The implications of Brexit on the foreign policy of European mini-states and their relation with the EU are significant and require careful consideration.

Finally, this subchapter explores the economic and political motivations behind the foreign policy choices of European mini-states within the EU. Understanding these driving factors is crucial for diplomats seeking to engage with these mini-states effectively.

In conclusion, the perception and reputation of European mini-states in global diplomacy have a profound impact on their foreign policy decisions. By examining their role within the EU, their influence on decision-making processes, and their ability to promote regional cooperation, diplomats can better understand the complexities and opportunities these mini-states present in the global diplomatic arena.

Implications of Perception and Reputation on Foreign Policy Objectives and Strategies

The foreign policy decisions of European mini-states are not only influenced by economic and political motivations but also by the perception and reputation they hold in global diplomacy. The way these mini-states are perceived by other nations and international organizations, including their own European Union (EU) counterparts, greatly impacts their foreign policy objectives and strategies. Understanding the implications of perception and reputation is crucial for diplomats and policymakers dealing with the foreign policy of European mini-states.

The perception of European mini-states can have significant consequences for their relations with the EU. A positive perception can lead to stronger cooperation and support from the EU, whereas a negative perception may result in skepticism and resistance. The impact of EU membership on the foreign policy of these mini-states is intricately linked to how they are perceived within the EU. A favorable reputation can grant them more influence in shaping EU foreign policy, whereas a negative reputation might limit their impact.

Comparative analysis of the foreign policy approaches of different European mini-states within the EU reveals the importance of perception and reputation. Mini-states with a strong reputation for diplomacy and mediation, for example, have a greater role in promoting regional cooperation and integration within the EU's foreign policy framework. Their positive reputation allows them to be seen as trustworthy mediators in international conflicts and negotiations, enhancing their influence and status.

However, challenges arise when European mini-states try to align their foreign policy with the EU's common stance. The perception and reputation of these mini-states can create obstacles in achieving complete alignment, as they strive to maintain their unique identities and interests. The implications of Brexit on the foreign policy of European mini-states and their relation with the EU further highlight the importance of perception and reputation. The way these mini-states navigate the post-Brexit landscape will shape their future perception and influence in global diplomacy.

Ultimately, the perception and reputation of European mini-states have a direct impact on their foreign policy decisions. The way they are perceived shapes their relations with the EU and other nations, influences their role in shaping EU foreign policy, and determines their effectiveness as mediators in international conflicts. Diplomats and policymakers must consider these implications to navigate the complex terrain of European mini-states' foreign policy within the EU and the global diplomatic arena.

How European Mini-States Leverage their Image for Diplomatic Success

In today's globalized world, the role of European mini-states in international diplomacy is often underestimated. These small territories, such as Monaco, San Marino, Andorra, and Liechtenstein, have managed to leverage their unique image to achieve diplomatic success on various fronts. This subchapter explores the driving factors behind their foreign policy choices and their impact on European Union (EU) relations.

One of the key factors that enable European mini-states to succeed diplomatically is their ability to navigate their relationship with the EU. Despite not being full EU members, they have managed to establish strong ties with the Union, often through bilateral agreements. These agreements allow mini-states to align their foreign policy with the EU's common stance, enabling them to have a say in decision-making processes. As a result, these mini-states can influence EU foreign policy, even if indirectly.

Furthermore, the comparative analysis of the foreign policy approaches of different European mini-states within the EU reveals interesting patterns. Despite their small size, these states have developed unique strategies to promote regional cooperation and integration within the EU's foreign policy framework. Their specialized knowledge and experience in certain areas, such as finance or tourism, make them valuable contributors to EU policies in these sectors.

The perception and reputation of European mini-states in global diplomacy also play a crucial role in their foreign policy decisions. These states are often seen as neutral and trustworthy mediators in international conflicts and negotiations. Their small size and lack of significant military capabilities give them a unique advantage in being perceived as honest brokers in resolving disputes.

However, European mini-states also face challenges in aligning their foreign policy with the EU's common stance. The implications of Brexit, for instance, have raised concerns about the future of their relations with the EU. Nevertheless, these states have shown resilience and adaptability in their foreign policy choices, finding new avenues for collaboration and cooperation, even in the face of uncertainty.

In conclusion, the driving factors behind the foreign policy choices of European mini-states within the EU are multifaceted. Their ability to leverage their image, navigate EU relations, and promote regional cooperation has enabled them to succeed diplomatically. As mediators in international conflicts and negotiations, these mini-states have proven their relevance in global diplomacy. Despite the challenges they face, their economic and political motivations continue to shape their foreign policy decisions and contribute to their overall success.

Conclusion: The Driving Factors: Economic and Political Motivations of European Mini-States' Foreign Policy

In this book, we have explored the driving factors behind the foreign policy decisions of European mini-states, with a focus on their economic and political motivations. Throughout our analysis, we have examined the unique position of these mini-states within the European Union (EU) and their impact on shaping EU foreign policy. We have also discussed the challenges and opportunities they face in aligning their foreign policy with the EU's common stance, the role they play in promoting regional cooperation and integration, and their reputation in global diplomacy.

One of the key findings of our research is that economic considerations play a significant role in the foreign policy decisions of European mini-states. These states often rely heavily on trade, tourism, and financial services, making economic stability and growth a top priority. As such, they carefully weigh their foreign policy choices to ensure they align with their economic interests, while also considering the potential impact on their relations with the EU and other international partners.

Furthermore, political motivations also shape the foreign policy approaches of European mini-states. These states often have unique political systems and cultural identities, which influence their foreign policy priorities. Some mini-states may seek to maintain their autonomy and independence, while others may prioritize close cooperation and integration with the EU. These political motivations, coupled with economic considerations, result in a diverse range of foreign policy approaches among the mini-states.

The EU membership of these mini-states has a profound impact on their foreign policy decisions. While EU membership provides them with access to a larger market and enhanced security, it also requires them to align their foreign policy with the EU's common stance. This alignment can present both opportunities and challenges, as mini-states must balance their own interests with those of the EU, while also navigating the complexities of EU decision-making processes.

Looking ahead, the implications of Brexit on the foreign policy of European mini-states and their relation with the EU are significant. As the UK's closest neighbors, these mini-states will face new challenges and opportunities in maintaining their own relationship with the EU and shaping its foreign policy decisions. Their role as mediators in international conflicts and negotiations may also be impacted, as the dynamics of global diplomacy undergo changes.

In conclusion, the economic and political motivations of European mini-states are crucial in understanding their foreign policy choices. As diplomats, it is essential to recognize the unique position of these mini-states within the EU and their influence on shaping EU foreign policy. By understanding their challenges, opportunities, and contributions, we can foster stronger diplomatic relations and cooperation within the European landscape.